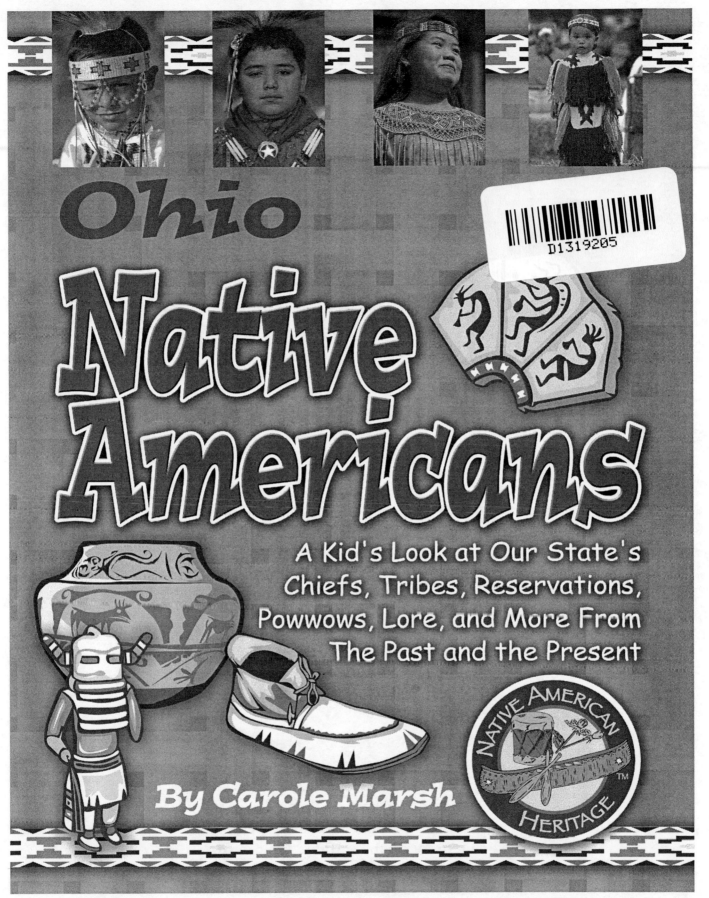

Ohio Native Americans

A Kid's Look at Our State's Chiefs, Tribes, Reservations, Powwows, Lore, and More From The Past and the Present

By Carole Marsh

Graphic Design: Lynette Rowe • Cover Design: Victoria DeJoy

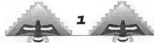

1

©2004 Carole Marsh/Gallopade International/www.gallopade.com/Ohio Indians A-Z

Published by

GALLOPADE™
INTERNATIONAL

800-536-2GET
www.gallopade.com

Gallopade is proud to be a member of these educational organizations and associations:

The National School Supply and Equipment Association (NSSEA)
American Booksellers Association (ABA)
Virginia Educational Media Association (VEMA)
Association of Partners for Public Lands (APPL)
Museum Store Association (MSA)
National Association for Gifted Children (NAGC)
Publishers Marketing Association (PMA)
International Reading Association (IRA)
Association of African American Museums (AAAM)

Native American Heritage™ Series

Native American
Big Activity Book

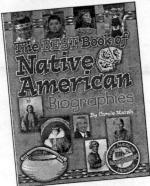

Native American
Biographies

Native American
Coloring Book

Native American
Heritage Book

Native American
Timeline

Ohio State Stuff™

My First Pocket Guide: Ohio

My First Book About Ohio

Ohio Coloring Book

The Big Ohio Reproducible Activity Book

Jeopardy: Answers & Questions About Our State

Ohio "Jography!": A Fun Run Through Our State

Ohio Gamebooks

Ohio Bingo Games

Ohio Illustrated Timelines

Ohio Project Books

Ohio Bulletin Board Set

Ohio PosterMap

Ohio Stickers

Let's Discover Ohio! CD-ROM

3

Word from the Author

Hello!

I hope you are as interested in North America's wonderful Indian heritage as I am!

Like most kids, I grew up thinking of Indians as the other half of Cowboys. Today, of course, we are getting a much clearer and more accurate picture of what the first peoples on our land were all about. These "facts" are much more fascinating than anything Hollywood can make up. And you probably won't find much of this information in your history textbook!

I am 1/16 Cherokee. This is something I am very proud of and happy about. My grandmother was 1/4 Cherokee. She had tan skin, long gray hair and a very Indian look – especially if I did something bad! Her maiden name was Carrie Corn. Of course, when she got married, she took her husband's name, so it was many years before I learned to appreciate the significance of my native heritage.

Today, I'm trying to make up for lost time by exploring my roots as deeply as I can. One of the most interesting things I've learned is how fascinating all of the Indian tribes are – in the past, the present and future!

As you read about "your" Indians, remember that all native peoples were part of an ever-changing network of time, ideas, power and luck — good and bad. This is certainly a history that is not "dead," but continues to change – often right outside our own back doors! – all the time.

Carole Marsh
She-Who-Writes

PS: Many references show different spellings for the same word. I have tried to select the most common spelling for the time period described. I would not want to be in an Indian spelling bee!

4

Adze

An Indian woodworking tool used to cut, scrape, or gouge; often used to hollow dugout canoes. Blades were made of stone, shell, bone or copper.

American Indian Mission

Allegheny Lenape, Canton; 17,000 members nationwide; annual festival in June.

Awl

An Indian's "needle." Often made from wood, thorns, bone, or metal, it was used to punch holes in skins so they could be sewn together.

Achsinnink

Lenni Lenape village of 1770 on the Hocking River. This Chippewa word means "at the place of the rough rock", or where it is hard to cross.

American Indian Lore Association

Logan; purpose is to study, interpret and preserve Indian lore; gives an annual Peace Pipe award; publishes *The Evanpaha*; has a museum and library; founded 1957.

Altar

A platform made of rocks or animal skulls; some had bowls, feathers, rattles, or skins on them. Indians prayed at these altars for things like good crops or expert hunting skills.

Arrow

A long, slender shaft made of reed, cane, or wood; pointed tip was attached to one end and split feathers to the other. Feathers helped the arrows fly straight.

Arrowhead

The pointed tip of an arrow, made of bone, antler, wood, or iron. Some tips had barbs that would embed themselves in flesh. These barbs made it difficult for an enemy to remove the arrowhead from a wound.

Artifacts

Early findings from the era of ancient native peoples in Ohio include obsidian spear points, incised pottery, copper ornaments, stone pipes and even seashells.

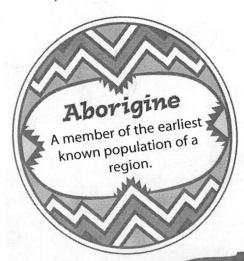

Aborigine

A member of the earliest known population of a region.

5

 **is for . . .**

Battle of Fallen Timbers

Near present-day Defiance. Where Miami Chief Little Turtle was defeated by Gen. "Mad" Anthony Wayne, marking the end of Indian resistance to white settlement in Ohio.

Band

A subdivision of an Indian tribe. In earlier times, a band was sometimes created when part of a tribe split off from the main group. The band also chose new leadership.

Black Hoof

Shawnee chief; fought the white man, but was later a friend to the Americans. Died at Wapakoneta in 1831.

Baskets

Some were woven and others were coiled. Baskets were made from roots, grasses, barks, and other natural materials.

Buckongahelas

Head chief of the Delaware (Lenni Lenape) Indians. At Presque Isle, he changed from fighting with the English to fighting against them. Signed a treaty at Greenville in 1795.

Bird Stones

Found in the Ohio area. Stones, carefully shaped into a bird. Possibly used in ceremonies or by Indian women in connection with marriage or pregnancy.

Bow

Made from wood, horn or bone. Ohio Indian children learned how to use bows. The bowstring was made from animal gut, rawhide or twisted vegetable fibers.

Bone

Animal bones were used by Ohio Indians to make buttons, whistles and other items.

Brandt, Joseph

Famous Mohawk chief who was born on the Ohio River in 1742 when his parents were on a hunting expedition.

C is for . . .

Copper
Used by Ohio Indians in its original state; later discovered they could pound into celts, tablets, bracelets and blades.

Chief
Leader of a tribe. Different titles meant different things. Some members were made chief because they owned deeds to land. Chieftainship was often inherited, usually from the mother!

Contact Period
What historians call the era in the 1500s when Native Americans first met Europeans. This meeting changed the lifestyle of the Ohio Indians more than anyone could ever have anticipated!

Coshocton
Ohio town named for a Delaware Indian chief; name means "finished or complete."

Cayuga
One of the five original nations of the Iroquois; moved to Ohio from New York after the American Revolution and together with other tribes became known as the Seneca of Sandusky (although there were few, if any Seneca there!).

Cat Nation
Nickname of the Erie Indians, whose name means "long tail," referring to the panther.

Clan
A tribal unit. Members are descended from the same ancestor.

Conus Mound
Marietta; built by the Adena Indians; now stands in Mound Cemetery where many early residents are buried.

Cult of the Dead
Early mound builders who moved into the Ohio Valley. Their mounds were used for burials.

Chillicothe
Site of a burial tomb mound lined with weapons and ornaments of beaten copper.

7

Dance

There were Indian dances for every occasion: war, peace, hunting, rain, good harvests, etc. Drums, rattles, and flutes of bone or reed provided the music. Dancers often chanted or sang while performing. Steps were not easy to learn and required consistent practice.

Descendants

The first Ohio Indians were descendants of primitive hunters who crossed the Bering Strait from Asia to what is now Alaska. At that time, glacial ice still covered most of North America. These people were the true discoverers of the "New World!"

Disease

Ohio Indians had no immunity to the diseases that white explorers, colonists and settlers brought to their lands. These diseases included smallpox, measles, tuberculosis and others, which ravaged the tribes in great epidemics that killed many, and sometimes all, members of a tribe.

Delaware Indians

Another name for the Lenni Lenape; came to the Muskingum Valley in Ohio to flee the domination of the Iroquois—the most important Algonquian confederacy. The English called them Delawares from their river. The French called them loups or "wolves."

Dyes

Made of lichens, berries, roots, bark, plants, and other natural materials by Indians in Ohio. Different colors were used depending on what materials were available and what objects were to be dyed.

Dishes

Made from clay, bark, wood, stone, and other materials, depending on what was available and what food they would be used for.

Dance of Fire

The Huron (Wyandot) performed a ritualistic dance called the Dance of Fire. Dancers would carry smoldering coals or heated stones in their mouths! They also plunged their arms into boiling water. They thought doing this would call up a spirit who would cure the sick.

Dreams

Important in the Indian tradition. It was believed that dreams were the "windows" to the soul. Many thought a person's hidden desires were expressed in dreams.

8

 **is for . . .**

Eagle

An animal used in many Indian ceremonies. Eagle feathers attached to war bonnets and shields communicated an Indian's rank in his tribe and what kinds of deeds he had done. Feathers also adorned rattles, pipes, baskets, and prayer sticks.

Eastern Shawnee

Historically associated with the Seneca who once lived in Ohio, but later moved to Kansas.

Erie

Tribe's name meant "long tail." Indians that once fished and hunted along the eastern shore of Lake Erie. Their name has been given to a Great Lake, counties in New York, Ohio and Pennsylvania and places in Colorado, Illinois, Kansas, Michigan, North Dakota, Tennessee, Ohio and New York, plus to a famous railroad and canal!

Earrings

Medicine men sometimes pierced male and female ears at special ceremonies. Earrings, which cost parents or relatives a significant amount, symbolized wealth and distinction. The more earrings that an Indian wore, the greater his honor. Some earrings measured 12 inches in length!

Events You Won't Want to Miss!

Traditional Pow Wow – April, Kent; Annual Moon When The Ponies Shed Powwow – May, Hilliard; Annual Competition Powwow – June, Cleveland; Annual Gathering of the People – July, Eaton; Annual Labor Day Weekend Powwow – September, Hilliard; Woodland Indian Celebration – October, Perrysburg; Atwood Lake Powwow – October, Atwood Lake Park.

English

In the 1800s, the U.S. government built boarding schools for Indian children throughout the nation. Children were forced to leave their homes and families to live at these schools. They were required to learn English and not speak their native languages.

Epidemics

Few Indians possessed immunity to the deadly diseases, like smallpox and measles, which European explorers and settlers brought to the New World. As a result, great population loss took place. Sometimes entire tribes became extinct. Epidemics sparked by Hernando De Soto's expedition are estimated to have killed 75% of the native population in the New World.

9

F is for . . .

Fetish

These small objects were thought to hold the spirit of an animal or a part of nature. A fetish could be an object found in nature, such as bone or wood, or it could be a carved object. The fetish was usually small enough to be carried in a small bag or on a cord. The making and use of a fetish was kept secret by its owner and only shared with the one who inherited it.

Fort Green Ville

Site where Indians eventually signed a treaty handing over more than 2/3 of present-day Ohio to the Americans.

Fort Hill State Memorial

Site of a prehistoric hilltop enclosure, possibly built by the Hopewell Indians.

Fire Drill

A device used by Indians to make fires which consisted of a stick and a piece of wood with a tight hole in it. The stick was twirled rapidly in the hole, creating friction that would ignite shredded grass or wood powder placed nearby to start a fire.

Farmers

Many Ohio Indians, ancient and modern, have farming ways! Even pre-contact Indians tilled and irrigated, raising many important crops. Corn, cotton, beans, squash, melons, sunflowers, gourds, pumpkins and tobacco are all native Indian crops!

Federal Recognition

The United States government's official acknowledgement of a group of Indians as a tribe that is eligible for government benefits, programs and funds.

Footwear

Ohio Indians wore different footwear depending on their tribe and environment. Moccasins were made mostly of animal skin. Sandals were made of rawhide or plant material.

Fort Ancient

Near Lebanon; 3 miles of earthen walls enclose nearly 100 acres of land. Built by early native peoples, probably for defense, along the Little Miami River. The Indians there once farmed the rich floodplains and foraged for fish, clams and wild edible plants. The museum there includes exhibits of the peoples who occupied the Fort Ancient site.

 # G is for . . .

Games

Adults played ball and other games of chance or skill. Indian children spun tops, fought pretend battles, did target-shooting, walked on stilts, played hide and seek, or competed to see who could hold their breath the longest!

Greentown

Delaware Indian village located on the Black Fork of the Mohican River in Ohio.

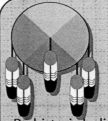

Go Visit Sun Watch!

Prehistoric Indian village and National Historic Landmark. See where Ohio's early Indian farmers settled 800 years ago. Archaeological excavations led to the reconstruction of their village. Here you can see how they lived, how they shaped the environment around them, the items they created and how scientists pieced together the artifacts excavated over more than 20 years.

Gens

Group of related members from different tribes.

Gathering

Native Americans gathered natural materials for food, fuel, baskets, clothing, and housing. American Indians tribes also hunted to meet basic needs. Even though some tribes planted crops, most did some kind of gathering.

Gorgets

Beautiful ornaments hung around the neck or from ears; their significance, if any, is unknown.

Gourds

Hollowed-out shell of a gourd plant's dried fruit which often grew into a specific shape. Indians raised many species of gourds. They were used for spoons, bowls, masks, rattles, and even storage.

Great Serpent Mound

Near Hillsboro in Adams County; resembles a large, partially-coiled snake. Stretches for almost 1/4 mile. Clenched in the serpent's jaws is an egg-shaped mound 30 feet wide! Built by the Adena people long before Christopher Columbus arrived. In 1900, Harvard College donated the mound to the Ohio Archaeological and Historical Society. A museum here exhibits material from the Adena culture.

11

Hatchet

A small, short-handled ax, primarily used as a tool, not as a weapon. When settlers moved in, stone hatchets were replaced with iron ones.

Hair

Indians used hair as a textile. Hair from bison, mountain sheep, elk, moose, deer, dog, rabbit, beaver, or even humans were used to weave cloth, make wigs, or stuff pillows, balls, dolls or drumsticks.

Horn and Hooves

Indians used animal horn to make spoons and dishes. Hooves were made into rattles and bird beaks were used for decoration.

Hopewell Culture

Early people who lived in the Ohio Valley from about 100 B.C. to A.D. 500. Anthropologists believe they had a layered society with a defined organization and code of conduct. Because of this, they could work together to build great earthenworks called mounds. They also had an extensive trade network from the Midwest to the eastern U.S. seacoast.

Historic Indian Museum

Piqua; restored 1829 home of federal Indian agent John Johnston. Contains artifacts of Native American tools, art, canoes, costumes and more. Describes the lifestyle of Ohio Indians after the white man came. Has a life-size diorama of Indians and French traders.

Hunters

Early Indian peoples were hunters who used wooden spears with stone points to kill many kinds of large mammals that are extinct today, such as mammoths and mastodons!

Hog Creek

1831 Shawnee village located in Allen County.

Horses

Spaniards brought the horse to America. At first, Indians were afraid of the horse or thought it was sacred. Later, Indians "broke" horses gently, often "hypnotizing" them with a blanket. Horses were used for transportation, trade, barter or payment. Some Indians ate horse meat in hopes of gaining the animal's power.

Huron

These Indians were powerful traders who lived on the Canada side of the Great Lakes. Iroquois invasions scattered the Huron and caused a series on migrations to the U.S. side of the lakes in the late 1600s that lasted into the 1700s. By 1842 they had sold their lands in the U.S. and were moved to Indian Territory. Their native name, Wyandot, used when talking about tribal members who relocated to the U.S.

Indian Raiding Parties

Ohio Indians did not give up their lands lightly. Between 1783 and 1790, they killed, wounded or took prisoner around 1,500 settlers trying to establish themselves along the Ohio River.

Indian Wars

Lasted 4 years along the Ohio River on the Indiana border. The Indians were fighting to keep their lands. They soundly defeated Gen. Josiah Harmar's untrained, poorly equipped militia in 1790. In 1791, they attacked Fort Recovery in the worst military defeat in an engagement with Indians in American history. But their last stand would eventually be in vain.

Indian Removal Act of 1830

This federal act gave President Andrew Jackson the power to relocate tribes east of the Mississippi to an "Indian Territory." The forced removal of the southeast Indians later became known as the "Trail of Tears."

Independence

Native American tribes are sovereign nations. That means they are independent. Some even issue their own passports! However, Native Americans are also considered citizens of the United States and enjoy all the rights and privileges of U.S. citizens.

Iroquois Nation

Powerful federation of six Indian tribes that were well established in the area of New York state. In 1656, they fought the Eries, then the Lenni Lenape and Wyandots, driving these Native Americans westward into the Ohio Valley. In the early 1700s, the Iroquois controlled many Indian tribes.

Indian

In 1493, Christopher Columbus called the native people he met in North America "Indians" because he mistakenly believed he had sailed to India! Today, this term includes the aborigines of North and South America.

Indian Ladder

Indians made ladders by trimming branches off a tree. Some were left at consistent intervals to provide steps.

Indian Tribes in Ohio

At one time or another, these tribes have lived in the state of Ohio:

Cayuga, Erie, Huron (Wyandot), Lenni Lenape (Delaware), Miami, Seneca, Shawnee

13

J is for . . .

Just So You Know . . .

Today you can find many Ohio Indians that follow some traditional ways. But there are also many who are entrepreneurs, doctors, lawyers, educators and even politicians! If you visit a reservation or cultural event, make sure you know visitor etiquette. Often dances are religious ceremonies and should be observed as such; religious dances should not be applauded. Photography, videotaping and drawing are all important issues – check with the tribe or individual before any is started.

Jesuits

Roman Catholic priests called Jesuits were among the first to meet and live with the North American Indians. Their writings, sent back to Europe, serve as one of today's best references to early Indian life.

Justice?

For hundreds of years, Native Americans have not received justice from federal and state governments. Native Americans have had nearly all their land taken away. Native Americans still have to fight for their rights in courts across the land.

Judicial Termination

Modern term to describe current efforts by various U.S. government agencies and officials (especially the judicial system) to legally decrease the sovereignty of independent Indian tribes.

Junqueindundeh

Huron village located on the Sandusky River around 1756.

Jet

Hard, black variety of lignite, a type of coal. Used by Ohio Indians to make face paint, small figures, or in jewelry.

 *is for . . .*

Knife

Made from various materials such as bone, reed, stone, wood, antler, shell, metal, or animal teeth (bear, beaver, etc.), knives were used as weapons but also creative handiwork.

Kill Site

An archaeological site where remains of many animals have been found along with human artifacts. Many kill sites have been useful to scientists in learning how ancient American Indians lived.

Killed Pottery

Pottery placed in a grave as an offering to the dead person was called killed pottery. A hole was formed in its base during creation. Often broken pottery was placed in a grave because Indians believed the spirit of the dead person would then be released and could travel.

Killbuck Town

Delaware Indian village located in Wayne County around 1764.

Knowledge

Knowledge is power. Native Americans shared knowledge with the first European settlers. Native Americans showed settlers how to plant crops, which plants were safe to eat, and other knowledge about the land.

Knots

Tied on bowstrings, spearhead and arrowhead lashings, snowshoes, and other items, knots were sometimes used to keep track of the days like a calendar—each knot equaled 1 day.

L is for . . .

Linguistic Families

There are 56 related groups of American Indian languages. A few of these speech families include Iroquoian, Algonquian, Siouan, Muskogean, Athapascan, and Wakashan.

Leggings

Both men and women wore cloth or skin covering, which were often decorated with quills, beads, or painted designs, for their legs.

Logan, John

Famous Iroquois (Mingo) chief. After some men had murdered his family, he and Chief Cornstalk began an uprising known as Dunmore's War. Refusing to sit at the peace council, he wrote a letter to Governor Dunmore. He read it in 1774 beneath an elm tree in Circleville, saying: "There runs not a drop of my blood in the veins of any living creature. This called on me for revenge. I have sought it; I have killed many; I have fully glutted my vengeance."

Lenni Lenape

What the Delaware Indians called themselves; means "real men." More common name used for the tribe today.

Little Turtle

Indian chief who helped combine the Miami, Shawnee and Delaware tribes into a united force to fight the white man's overtaking of their homelands. After his defeat and signing a treaty, he proclaimed, "I am the last to sign it and I will be the last to break it." He kept his word.

Leatherlips

A chief of the Ohio Huron who was sentenced to death by Tecumseh because of his friendship with whites. He received a piece of bark with a war club on it to indicate he would be executed. This took place on the Scioto River near Columbus in 1810. He was killed by a war club's blow as he knelt beside his open grave, chanting his death song. A granite monument was erected in his memory in 1888 by the Wyandot Club of Columbus.

Land Loss

Native Americans lost their land in many ways. Conflicts with other tribes, colonization, European settlement, treaties, and removal took away Indian lands.

Lance

Spear used for hunting and war. The hunting lance had a short shaft and a broad, heavy head. The war lance was light and had a long shaft.

Lewistown

Shawnee and Seneca settlement that is the site of this present-day Ohio town, named for Shawnee chief, Captain Lewis.

16

 **is for . . .**

Mound Builders State Memorial

Glenford; museum centered around an original flint pit, including 2 Hopewell quarries.

Miamisburg Mound

Located near Dayton; one of the largest conical mounds in eastern North America.

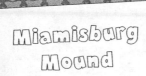

Mound City Group National Monument

Chillicothe; 240 acre park preserving 23 burial mounds and 2 Hopewell earthen enclosures plus a museum on the Hopewell trade network.

Mound of Pipes

Got its name from the 200 large effigy pipes which are now housed in the British Museum.

Mica Grave Mound

Filled with glittering mica; today you can see a cutaway section that shows how burial mounds were constructed.

Moccasins

Indian shoes made of animal skin.

Medicine Man

A person who got the power to heal the sick through a secret means, usually from a dream or visions.

Miami

Algonquian Indians who lived in western Ohio; formed a crucial alliance with the Shawnee. They called themselves Twightwees, a name that came from the cry of the crane. Worshiped the sun and thunder. Lived in houses covered with bark or rush mats. By 1827, they had sold all their Ohio lands and moved to Kansas. Three Ohio rivers and a county plus places in Ohio, Indiana, California, Oklahoma, Missouri and Texas are named for them, but not places in Florida!

Nation

There are many Indian nations located within the United States, such as the Alleghenny Nation. Indian nations are called nations because their governments and laws are independent of and separate from the U.S. government. The federal government must have "government to government" relations with these Indian nations, just as it would with foreign nations, like England or Spain.

Nomadic

A way of life in which people frequently moved from one location to another in search of food. "Seminomadic" people had permanent villages, but left them in certain seasons to hunt, fish, or gather wild plant foods.

Newark Mounds

A series of Indian mounds and enclosures located in Licking County, Ohio. The Mound Builders Museum is also located here.

Names

Indian names were often changed during one's lifetime. These names could be derived from events that happened during the person's birth, childhood, adolescence, war service, or retirement from active tribal life. Some names came from dreams, some were inherited, and sometimes names were stolen or taken in revenge. Today some Indians maintain old, traditional Indian names, while others take modern names. Since settlers often did not read or write Indian languages, they recorded Indian names phonetically (as they "sounded"). Thus Indian names were often misspelled.

November

In 1990, President George Bush approved a joint resolution designating November 1990 "National American Indian Heritage Month." Similar proclamations have been issued each year since 1994.

National Museum of the American Indian

The Smithsonian's National Museum of the American Indian on the National Mall in Washington, D.C., symbolizes a deeper understanding between America's first citizens and those who have come to make these shores their home.

Notched Plates

Stone plates that had notches in them have been found in Ohio Indian mounds. They may have been used to grind paint pigments. Some of the plates have intricate bird, snake or other designs.

18

 **is for . . .**

Ohio Mound Builders

About 2,000 years ago a wave of migrating people came to our area. They were the first of many groups to be known as the Mound Builders, for the earthenworks they created. Were mainly hunters and fishers, but did some farming. They left behind a dramatic record of their existence — more than 10,000 earthen mounds! Sometimes built high earthen walls around their villages, possibly for defense. They vanished long before the first white explorers reached Ohio.

Ohio

From the Iroquois word O-he-yo which means "great or beautiful river."

Oil

Indians extracted oil from the many layers of fat that came with fresh bear meat. The fat was boiled down in earthen pots to produce the oil, which was stored in gourds and pots. The oil was used for cooking and even beautifying the body! Indians would mix red pigment with the oil, add the fragrances of cinnamon and sassafras, and rub it all over their bodies.

Obsidian

Black volcanic glass used by Indians to make spear and arrow points. Obsidian artifacts found in Ohio mounds must have gotten to Indians here through trade, since this glass is not naturally found here.

Omaha

One of the main Siouan-speaking tribe. They moved west from Ohio, following the rivers.

"Old Britain"

Miami Indian Chief; got his nickname because he was so loyal to the British. Was killed at Pickawillany during a surprise raid.

Ohio Indian Art Museum

Located at the Moundbuilders State Memorial in Newark. Prehistoric Indian art museum and historic site depicting the Great Circle Earthworks. The first museum in America devoted to prehistoric Native American art.

 **is for . . .**

Powwow

The original form of the word meant "medicine man." Medicine men would often use noise motion and confusion to scare away harmful spirits and cure people. It was also a gathering to talk about political matters. Today, the powwow is an event where Indians gather to sing, perform ceremonial dances, and share cultural pride and traditions.

Pokagon, Simon

A chief of the Potawatomi Indians. He attended Oberlin College in Ohio, spoke 5 languages, and was considered the most educated Indian of his time. He wrote many articles, published a book and managed the affairs of his tribe.

Pickawillany

Miami Indian village at Loramie Creek and Great Miami River. Site of an important battle in 1752 during the French and Indian Wars. The village was a trading post visited by both French and English. Because the Miami supported the English, French commander Charles Langlade and some Indians stormed the village, plundered the storerooms, then burned the fort to the ground.

Pemmican

Indian food made of animal meat, which was dried in the sun, pounded together with fat and berries. The mixture was packed into skin bags and used primarily while on the trail.

Paint

Indians used many natural materials to make paint, like clay mixed with oil or grease. Yellow "paint" was made with the gall bladder of a buffalo! Why did they paint their faces or bodies? Indians used paint to look scary or beautiful, to disguise themselves, or to protect their skin from sunburn or insect bites. Indians often applied red paint because it symbolized strength and success.

Pearls

Have been found in Ohio Indian mounds; probably traded with Gulf Coast Indians.

Papoose

An American Indian infant aged between birth and one year is called a papoose. A papoose spent most of his or her days snugly wrapped in a kind of cradle made of skins or bark and a wooden frame that hung on the mother's back. This sturdy frame also allowed a mother to lean her papoose against a tree or rock within sight as she worked.

Pontiac

A great Ottawa Indian chief who organized many of the Great Lakes tribes in an effort to drive the British from Indian territory. Born in Ohio in 1712.

Pottery

Indian pottery was made from built-up spirals of clay that were molded or paddled, or a combination of the two methods. Most pottery served as cooking vessels.

 **is for . . .**

Quillwork

Indians used the quills of porcupine or birds to make a type of embroidery. Quills were dyed with juice from berries and other materials. When they were ready to be used, the quills were either mashed with teeth or softened with hot water and flattened with rocks. The quills were then laced into moccasins, shirts, pipe covers, and other items. Beads which Indians received by trading with settlers eventually replaced quillwork.

Quality

Native American arts and crafts are known for their excellent craftsmanship and striking designs. This work is often influenced by things found in nature especially plants and animals.

Quiver

Case used to hold arrows; made of woven plant materials or animal skins.

Quirt

A short riding whip with a wood, bone, or horn handle.

Quarry Site

A location where Indians went for workable stone such as flint and made stone tools.

21

R is for . . .

Rain Dancing

The rain dance ceremony, performed to encourage rainfall, was common among Indian religions because good weather is vital for a successful harvest. Rainmakers were in tune with nature; there are actual reported cases of Indians producing or preventing rain!

Roots

Indians used plant roots for food, medicine, dye, baskets, cloth, rope, salt, flavoring, and just to chew!

Rattles

Indians of Ohio made rattles from bird beaks, animal hooves, bones, pods, seashells, turtle shells and other animal parts. The rattles are used in ceremonies.

Rawhide

Untanned animal hide. The "green" hide was stretched on the ground or over a frame. Flesh and fat were removed. The skin was dried, washed, then buried with wood ashes which made the hair come off. Used by the Ohio Indian to make drumheads, lash lodge poles, mend broken objects and in many other ways.

Revolution!

During the War for Independence, the British hoped to hold onto their territory west of the Alleghenies with the help of their Indian allies. But Gen. George Rogers Clark secured Ohio and other lands for the Americans.

Red Thunder

Sioux chief who fought at Sandusky, Ohio.

Reservations

The U.S. government set aside, or "reserved," land for the Indians. These reservations originally served as a sort of prison during the beginning stages of Indian removal. At that time, reservations provided the government with some control over Indian activity and residency. This land was usually considerably less desirable land than the Indians' native territories. Today's reservations are lands that are tribally held, yet protected by the government.

Roundhead

Ohio Indian town named for a Wyandot chief.

22

S is for . . .

Sign Language

A way for Indians to communicate with others from a tribe whose language they did not speak.

Shaman

Medicine man and spiritual leader who was supposed to have special healing power from another world.

Shawnee

Indians who migrated north to Ohio from Kentucky and North Carolina. Their seat of power in Ohio was a large village near the mouth of the Scioto River. They formed an important alliance with the Miamis. Their name mean "southerners." Their most famous chief was Tecumseh.

Salem

1781 Moravian Lenni Lenape village, located near Port Washington; was abandoned the same year.

Sweatlodge

Structure used for ritual purification by sweating from exposure to very hot fires or hot steam from pouring water over hot stones. Also called a sweathouse, for some tribes also doubling as clubhouses.

Secawgo

In 1807, this Potawatomi band visited the Indian meeting held at Greenville, Ohio.

Sacred Bundles

A group of objects treasured by a tribe. They were well-guarded and often taken into battle. The items were publicly shown only on very important occasions.

Salt Lick

Delaware Indian village at the site of a salt works in 1796; today's Warren, Ohio.

Schoenbrunn

Located on the Tuscarawas River near today's New Philadelphia. Mission established in 1772 by the Moravians where they converted many Lenni Lenape to Christianity and taught Indian children at Ohio's first schoolhouse. Former town of the Munsee Indians. During the Revolution, the Indians were forced to move to Sandusky. In 1782, the village was burned.

Signals

Indian signs made with a pony, blanket, mirror, smoke, fire-arrow or other item to communicate over long distances.

Sachem

The supreme Indian ruler of an area where there are many related tribes.

 **T** *is for . . .*

Treaty of Green Ville

1795; the Indians ceded their Ohio lands (almost 2/3 of the present-day state!) to the United States.

Toledo War

1835-1842. Indian Ohio and Michigan boundary dispute.

Treaty of Fort Stanwix

1768; established the Ohio River as the "permanent" border between Indian country to the northwest and white settlement to the south and east. About 60,000 Indians lived in the Great Lakes region at the time of this treaty.

Temple Mounds

The earthenworks of mound builders in the Ohio Valley. They were erected as substructures for their wooden temples.

Tarhe

Noted Wyandot chief also called Monsieur Grue by the French and Crane by the English. One of the chiefs who fought at the Battle of Fallen Timbers in Ohio. When 70 years old, led his warriors in the War of 1812. As chief priest of his tribe, he kept the calumet which bound the tribes north of the Ohio River in a confederation. Died at Cranetown, Ohio in 1816.

Tomahawk

A club, axe or hammer used to chop wood, drive stakes in the ground or as a weapon.

Tracking

To follow a trail by finding a sign such as a broken blade of grass, a moved stone or moccasin track. Indians learned to trail as children, so that they could find food, track enemies and disguise their own signs.

Teeth

Ohio Indians hung teeth on cords to make necklaces.

Tribe

A group of Indians with shared culture, history, original territory, ancestry, social organization, and governmental structure. A tribe may contain several bands of Indians.

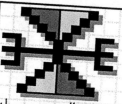

Thunderbird

A mythological Indian figure, as well as a part of the constellations for many Indians. Thunderbird mythology is mostly different from tribe to tribe, in general either coexisting with ancestors as an actual bird, or appearing as a spiritual nature god. The Thunderbird was good to the people in either case. Much mythology ties the thunderbird with thunder, lightning and storms.

Tecumseh

Shawnee chief who tried to create a great Indian state in the Ohio Valley and Great Lakes region by uniting many tribes under one leader. Born in 1768 near today's Springfield in a village called Piqua, later destroyed. A great leader, he opposed the white man's takeover of native lands, even forbidding the U. S. government from buying land from a single Indian tribe, saying that the land belonged to all tribes.

24

U is for . . .

U.S. Army

Many Native Americans have fought bravely for the United States Army. Many have also given their lives for a country that was not always accepting of them.

Unique

Each and every tribe has its own unique customs, language, and traditions.

U.S. Bureau of Indian Affairs

Provides public services such as law enforcement, land records, economic development, and education to Indians. Known for mismanagement and ethical problems.

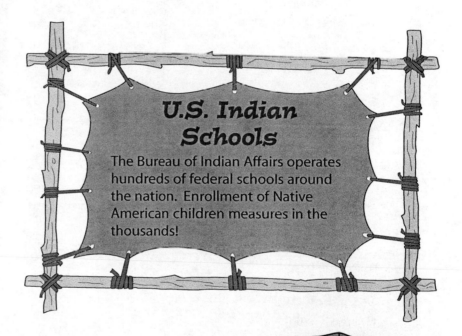

U.S. Indian Schools

The Bureau of Indian Affairs operates hundreds of federal schools around the nation. Enrollment of Native American children measures in the thousands!

U.S. Indian Reorganization Act

Passed by Congress in 1934, the act authorized Indian tribes to establish and conduct their own governments, and to form businesses.

U.S. President

Once called Great White Father by Indians.

U.S. Colonists

Called Long Knives or Big Knives by early Indians, who also called English explorers "Coat Men."

U.S. Indian Wars

The U.S. War Department has compiled an official list of "Indian Wars" that occurred in the United States. Over 50 wars were fought between the U.S. and the Indians during the period of 1790-1850.

25

 **is for . . .**

Vessels

Indians carried water in special gourds shaped liked bottles, called water vessels.

Village Councils

These were held in the town (council) house and occurred to discuss and decide important matters. Harmony and agreement was essential to tribal unity. Rather than vote on issues, they were discussed until everyone was satisfied. Anyone who wanted to could speak freely. Everyone did not always agree on the outcome, but everyone avoided conflict by pushing their case.

Vegetable Dyes

Indians could not buy color from the store like we can today. Instead, they created many different colors from the things they found on earth like plants, flowers, shrubs, trees, roots, and berries. They made beautiful and unique reds, oranges, yellows, greens, browns, and violets. These dyes were used for baskets, pottery, weaving, body makeup, and clothing.

Vanport Flint Ridge

9,000 years ago, Indians from all across the North American continent prized the red, blue, green, yellow and pink flint found in southeastern Licking and northwest Muskingum County. The shallow quarries where Indians once dug are still visible on the ridge. Today, it is used in making jewelry.

Villages

Many Ohio Indians lived in villages! Villages were formed around different clans or bands within the tribe, but could also contain different clans living together. Villages were usually permanent settlements, although semi-nomadic tribes have been known to migrate between permanent villages.

Vesperic Indians

Indian tribes located in the United States.

 **is for . . .**

War Bonnet

Special headdress worn into battle, often adorned with feathers.

War Pony

Horse, often painted with colorful paint and ridden into battle.

Wyandots

This is the name for the group of Huron Indians that relocated to the United States from Canada. They later fled from the Iroquois to present-day Marion, Crawford and Wyandot counties in Ohio.

Wampum

Algonquian word for "white." This described beads or strings of beads made of clam or whelk shells. They were used in trade between the Indians and settlers. In 1640, counterfeit wampum was made!

White Eyes

Delaware Indian chief who lived near today's Zanesville around 1776. Tried to keep his tribe neutral in wars with whites. Finally was forced to lead his people in battle. He said he would go before them and be the first to fall so he would not be able to witness their destruction. He died of smallpox before that could happen.

Whistle

Indians from Ohio made them from the wing bones of birds. The whistles made the sound of the bird the bones came from! Used to communicate, signal, sound an alarm or even flirt with a maiden!

War Club

A weapon made of stone, bone, or wood in the shape of a club.

White Man

Indians generally called them Pale Face, a name the white men themselves suggested!

War Dance

Indian braves danced this before going into battle. The dance was a way of assembling the braves and getting them to commit to the fight ahead.

X Y Z are for...

Xenophobe

A xenophobe is someone who is afraid of foreign people, their customs and cultures, or foreign things. Many of the first European settlers were afraid of Native American cultures.

You Bet!

Some Native Americans say that Casinos make a lot of money. Others say that too many people have a gambling problem. In the 1980s and 1990s, many tribes discussed whether or not gambling casinos should be allowed. Now that many casinos have been built across the country, the debate has switched to how it should be controlled.

Zounds!

Between 1871 and 1913, at least 98 traditional agreements between tribes and the United States were negotiated and 96 of them were ratified by Congress. Each agreement remains as law (unless changed by a later agreement)!

ZZZZZ...

Shamans and medicine men were not the only people who had access to the spirit world. Indians believed that people could make contact with spirits every night in their dreams! Dreamers could travel back to the time of man's creation or far ahead into their own futures. They also believed that dreams contained warnings or commands from the spirits. Many tribes felt that they had to act out their dreams as soon as they awoke. If an Indian dreamed about bathing, for example, he would run to his neighbors' houses first thing in the morning, and his neighbors would throw kettles full of cold water over him.

Y... Or, "Why?"

1. Why do you think Indian warriors carried charms with them? Some Indian medicines have been scientifically proven to have true healing power and are still used today. Do you think their charms had any real power to help them win battles?
2. Why do you think the American government kept relocating Indians onto reservations and then making the reservations smaller and smaller?
3. Why did Indians use items such as a pipe in ceremonies? What kinds of symbolic objects do we use in ceremonies today?
4. Why and how did Indians use natural materials in creative ways?
5. Many Indian tribes are running successful businesses on their reservations today. There is one industry that many tribes are making a lot of money at. Do you know what this is? Hint:"I'll bet you do!"

Which Famous Native American Am I?

Solve the puzzle!

Down

1. This Shoshone woman joined Lewis and Clark as their guide and translator and helped make the expedition a success! Hint: She has 4 "a"s in her name!

4. This man gave the Cherokee their first alphabet so that they could write. Until then, they communicated only by speaking and drawing pictures. Hint: A famous ancient tree also has the same name!

5. He was one of the fiercest of Indian warriors! He fought against white settlers in Arizona and New Mexico to keep his people from being pushed off their lands. Hint: Jump!

Word Bank

Black Elk   Crazy Horse   Sitting Bull   Sequoia
Sacajawea   Chief Joseph   Geronimo   Pocahontas

Across

2. A legend says that this brave Algonquian woman saved the life of Englishman John Smith. Hint: Disney produced a movie about her.

3. He fought at Little Bighorn when he was only 13! He was also a wise "shaman" who saw visions and could advise people. Hint: Part of his name is an animal with antlers!

6. He was a great Sioux warrior who won the battle against General Custer at Little Bighorn in 1876. Hint: His horse was not crazy!

7. A leader of the Lakota (Sioux) tribe who lived on the Standing Rock Reservation in North Dakota after the battle of Little Bighorn. He tried to make conditions better for his people there, so the U.S. government called him a "troublemaker." Hint: He did not sit all the time!

8. A wise and brave chief of the Nez Percé who tried to bring his people to Canada to escape war. He said, "From where the sun now stands, I will fight no more forever." Hint: His father's name was "Old Joseph."

Different Ways for Different Indians!

North American Indian tribes are divided into different areas. In each of these areas, tribes shared common ways of living with each other. They might make similar arts or crafts, they might eat the same foods, or they might have had the same beliefs. These activities are all part of their "culture." Each area had its own culture, which was different from the tribes in all the other areas.

Below is a map of all the different groups of Indian tribes in North America. Color each area with a different color. You will see a colorful picture of how Native Americans can all be called "Indians" but still have very different cultures!

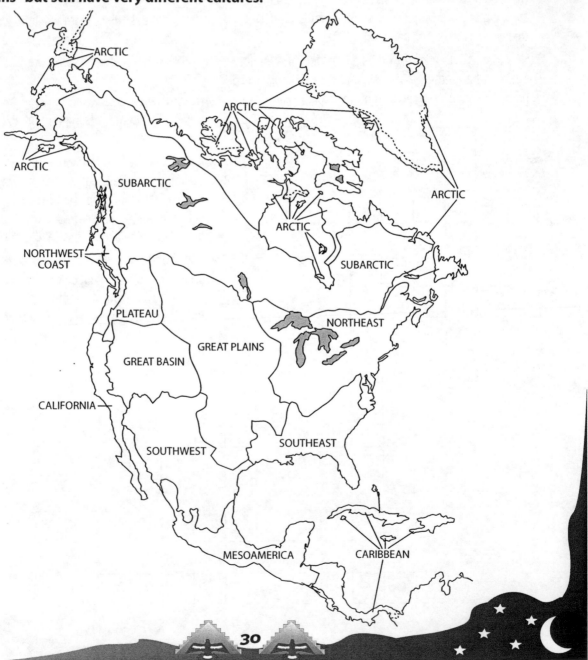

©2004 Carole Marsh/Gallopade International/www.gallopade.com/Ohio Indians A-Z

Celebration!

Powwows are big festivals where Native Americans gather to sing, dance, and eat together. It is a time to celebrate and show pride in their culture. Powwows can last from one afternoon to several days. The Indians dress in native costumes and dance ancient dances to the beating of drums.

Artists sell their arts and crafts. You might be able to buy some real Native American food cooked on an open fire. Native Americans go to powwows to be with each other, share ideas, and just have fun! Most powwows are also open to people who are not Indian. It's a great place to learn about Native American culture!

If you went to a powwow this weekend, what do you think you would see? What do you think might NOT be there? Circle the objects you think you would see at a powwow. Put an X through those you probably won't see.

©2004 Carole Marsh/Gallopade International/www.gallopade.com/Ohio Indians A-Z

Make an Indian Weaving!

Many Native Americans used weaving to create useful things like sashes (belts), bags, mats, and blankets. They used animal hair to make yarn, and dyed the yarn with natural dyes from fruits and other plants. They also used some plant fibers, like cotton, to make weaving thread.

Weave a small Native American mat of your own. Use different colors of yarn to create a beautiful pattern in your weaving. Place a favorite object on the mat or hang it on your wall!

Prepare the "loom"
Cut a piece of cardboard 5 inches wide and 6 inches long. Along the two 5-inch sides (the "short" sides), have an adult cut slits 1/4 inch deep. These slits should be 1/2 inch apart from each other. So, on each short side you will have 9 slits.

Directions:
1. Take a long piece of yarn and bring it from the back through the first slit (the one next to the edge of the cardboard.) The end of the yarn will hang down behind the cardboard.

2. Bring the yarn right across the front of the cardboard to the slit opposite the one your yarn came through.

3. Now bring the yarn under the back of the cardboard and then up again through the second slit.

4. Repeat #2 and #3, until you have 9 strands of yarn across the front of your cardboard!

5. Then cut the yarn and tie the two loose ends in the back of the cardboard.

6. Take another piece of yarn and start feeding it through the 9 strands, going over one, under the next over the next, etc. When you get to the end, pull the yarn behind the cardboard and around to the front, and begin again. This time, whatever strand you went over, go under. And whatever strand you went under, go over.

7. Repeat this pattern until the front of your cardboard in covered. Then cut the yarn in the back of the cardboard, and trim it to create a fringe for your mat!

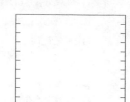

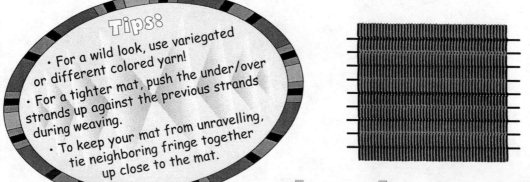

Tips:
- For a wild look, use variegated or different colored yarn!
- For a tighter mat, push the under/over strands up against the previous strands during weaving.
- To keep your mat from unravelling, tie neighboring fringe together up close to the mat.

Finders Keepers?

Native Americans have many buried treasures. For hundreds of years, special objects would sometimes be buried with Native Americans, or maybe they would just be lost. Archeologists used to dig for interesting artifacts in old Native American gravesites. They would keep the Native American bones or the arrowheads, rattles, masks and other objects that they found. But this made the Native Americans feel like they were being robbed.

In 1990, the U.S. government passed a law that said that no one could look for or take these Native American objects anymore. And whoever had any already had to give them back to the people they belonged to. This is called repatriation

Help the archeologist return the artifact to a Native American.

FINISH

START

Fast Fact

An artifact is an object that was made by people a long time ago for some useful purpose.

Busy Hands!

Before modern times, Native Americans didn't have stores where they went to buy things. They made everything they needed.

What did Indians make with their own hands? Use the Word Bank and pictures to find out!

Word Bank

blanket	moccasins	arrows	pottery	canoe
mat	food	jewelry	pouch	box

_ _ _ _ _ _ _ _ _ _ 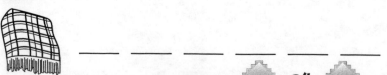 _ _ _ _ _ _ _ _ _ _

_ _ _ _ _ _ _ _ _ _ 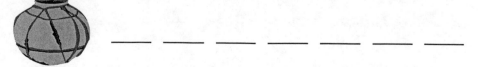 _ _ _ _ _ _ _ _ _ _

_ _ _ _ _ _ _ _ _ _ _ _ _ _ _ _ _ _ _ _

_ _ _ _ _ _ _ _ _ _ _ _ _ _ _ _ _ _ _ _

_ _ _ _ _ _ _ _ _ _ _ _ _ _ _ _ _ _ _ _

_ _ _ _ _ _ _ _ _ _ _ _ _ _ _ _ _ _ _ _

_ _ _ _ _ _ _ _ _ _ _ _ _ _ _ _ _ _ _ _

_ _ _ _ _ _ _ _ _ _ _ _ _ _ _ _ _ _ _ _

American Indians Today

Beginning with the first letter of each group of letters, cross out every other letter to discover some new words. You may not have heard of these before, but you can read all about them!

1. Many Indians live on these, but many more do not!

TRYELSDEBRNVJAOTPIPOWNASX

_____

2. Many Indians have been poor for a long time because for many years the government took away their lands and their ability to make a living.

TPKOOVWEBRNTXYA

_____

3. Many Indians have been studying hard at school and going to college in order to earn more money. Education helps the Indians make their lives better. These Native Americans are working to become:

TSJUMCBCFEYSMSOFPUVL

_____

4. This is a big term that means Native Americans have worked hard to get the U.S. government to let them rule themselves. This means that they have their own laws and make their own decisions. They are like a separate country inside the U.S.! Now, try and see if you can get your parents to give you the same thing!

TSGENLBF   JDGEETSEWRAMCIHNUAKTYIKOTNU

_____

Fast Fact
What do Indians work as today?

- doctors
- nurses
- factory workers
- artists
- lawyers
- actors

The same kinds of jobs any American might work at!

35

Native Americans Move to the City!

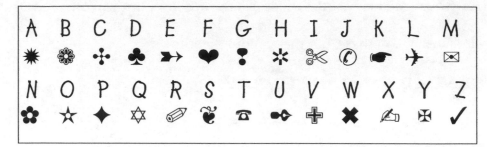

Solve the code to discover the mystery words!

A	B	C	D	E	F	G	H	I	J	K	L	M
✳	❀	♣	♧	➵	♥	❗	✳	✂	✆	☛	✈	✉

N	O	P	Q	R	S	T	U	V	W	X	Y	Z
❁	☆	◆	✡	✏	❦	☎	➝	✚	✖	✍	✠	✔

1. During the 1950s and 1960s, the American government paid Indians to leave their homes on reservations and move to cities to get jobs. If cities are sometimes called urban areas, then these brave Indians were called:

___ ___ ___ ___ ___   ___ ___ ___ ___ ___ ___ ___

2. Many Indians chose to stay on their reservations and not move to the city. They thought that if they moved to the city, they would lose the way of life that their parents and ancestors had taught. These Indians called themselves:

___ ___ ___ ___ ___ ___ ___ ___ ___ ___ ___   ___ ___ ___ ___ ___ ___ ___

3. Native Americans who moved to cities lived close to each other. They tried to keep their way of life as much as possible. They did not want to forget their religion, native art, or music. They did not want to lose their:

___ ___ ___ ___ ___ ___ ___

4. Are you afraid of heights? Many people are. The Mohawk Indians are not! Many of them work hundreds of feet above the city to build steel frames for skyscrapers. People who do this work above the city are:

___ ___ ___ ___ ___   ___ ___ ___ ___ ___ ___ ___

5. Today urban Indians and reservation Indians come together to celebrate their culture. They share ideas and stories. They dance and beat drums. They make and sell Indian jewelry. During these celebrations, Indians remember how much they have to be proud of! These big parties are called

___ ___ ___ ___ ___ ___ ___